ROBOT CRACKERS

BY
JONNY ZUCKER

ILLUSTRATED BY
ENZO TROIANO

Titles in Full Flight With Attitude

Badger Publishing Limited
Oldmedow Road, Hardwick Industrial Estate,
King's Lynn PE30 4JJ
Telephone: 01438 791037

www.badgerlearning.co.uk

2 4 6 8 10 9 7 5 3 1

Robot Safe Crackers ISBN 978-1-84691-662-5

First edition © 2009
This second edition © 2015

Text © Jonny Zucker 2009
Complete work © Badger Publishing Limited 2009

Series Editor: Jonny Zucker
Publisher: David Jamieson.
Editor: Danny Pearson
Design: Fi Grant
Cover illustration: Enzo Troiano

ROBOT SAFE CRACKERS

CONTENTS

Badger
LEARNING

CHAPTER 1
NEWS INFO

Tyler was playing Alien Smash 4 on his computer.

His sister Gail was working on her kick-boxing moves.

"It's such a sunny day," called their mum from the kitchen.

"You two should be outside enjoying the sun."

"In a minute!" replied Tyler.

"In a minute!" replied Gail.

"No way!" groaned Tyler as Alien Star Command destroyed his Human Power Ship.

He exited Alien Smash 4 and looked at the day's news.

"Check this out," he said looking up from his computer screen.

"What is it?" asked Gail. She stopped her kick-boxing practice and walked across the room. She looked at the computer screen:

"Another bank was robbed today by the gang who use robots.

As with all of the other robberies the robots stopped the CCTV cameras working, so there are no CCTV pictures.

The gang broke into the bank's safe and cleared out all of its money.

The police got to the scene too late. The money and the robots were gone."

SHOCK ROBBERY IN A BANK MADE BY A GROUP OF UNATTENDED

"Robot thieves?" said Gail, "weird!"

"Yeah," nodded Tyler, "totally weird."

What they did not know was that things were going to get a whole lot weirder.

CHAPTER 2
THE SMASH

Two days later, Tyler and Gail were out shopping with their mum.

"How about a super size drink and a serious snack?" asked Tyler.

"No way!" replied Mum. "I have got to go to the hairdressers. Meet me in the bank in an hour."

Tyler sighed. "Whatever," he replied.

Tyler and Gail went to a skateboard shop and checked out some boards.

Then they went to a music store and looked at some hip hop CDs.

"Let's go to the bank now," said Gail when they had finished in the record store.

They crossed the street and walked into the bank. There was no sign of Mum. Tyler checked his watch. They were fifteen minutes early.

The bank was busy. They sat down on a bench.

They had just started talking about the outdoor hip hop gig they were going to at the weekend, when there was suddenly a massive crashing sound.

Hundreds of bits of glass flew across the room.

Tyler and Gail put their hands over their heads to stop themselves being hit by glass.

Lots of people screamed and the bank filled up with a grey mist.

"EVERYONE ON THE GROUND!" shouted a cold, metallic voice.

Tyler and Gail looked at the bank's
doorway.

Through the mist, they saw that all of
the bank's windows had been smashed
out.

And the voice was coming from a tall,
steel robot.

CHAPTER 3
LOCK IN

"This way!" hissed Tyler, grabbing Gail's arm.

They ran behind a pillar and peeked out.

There were five robots in the bank and a man dressed in a grey suit.

The man was controlling the robots with what looked like a TV remote control flicker.

The robots had already smashed the CCTV cameras and thrown them on the floor.

Everyone in the bank was lying on the floor. People looked terrified, even the bank's security guards.

The man in the grey suit pressed some more buttons.

The robots began to smash their way through a solid steel wall towards the bank's safe.

"We have to stop them!" whispered Tyler.

"Are you mad?!" hissed Gail.

Tyler put a finger to his lips.

"Come on!" he said.

Making sure the man did not see them,
they kept low and ran along a wall.

When the man looked the other way,
they scrambled over the bank's counter.

There were six of the bank's workers
lying on the ground.

"Where is the bank's main computer?" whispered Tyler to one of the bank's workers.

She was lying face down and sobbing. She looked up and frowned at Tyler.

"What are you doing?" she whispered, "you will get us all killed."

"Just show me the computer!" ordered Tyler.

The woman pointed to a laptop.

"What's the pass code?" whispered Tyler.

"T7 84 Z," she replied.

Tyler punched in the code and got to work.

Gail kept a look out.
The robots were nearly at the door of the safe.

Tyler worked very fast.

He made a few mistakes but after a few seconds he understood how the bank's safe locking system worked.

"Hurry up!" hissed Gail.

Tyler hit the few last keys and suddenly there was a loud beeping sound from the safe.

"EXTRA SECURITY LOCK ON SAFE!" boomed one of the robots.

"NOT ABLE TO GAIN ACCESS!"

Gail gave Tyler a thumbs-up, but at that second, the man in the grey suit jumped over the counter.

And the first people he saw were Tyler and Gail.

CHAPTER 4
ROBOT WARS

"What are you doing?" screamed the man.

"Trying to stop you!" shouted Tyler.

"STOP ME?" roared the man. "You are just a kid!"

The man pressed a button on his flicker and a robot appeared.

"Take these two to the van and keep them inside," he shouted.

"I will deal with them later."

The robot grabbed Tyler and Gail by the arms and dragged them towards the doors, past lots of frightened people who were lying on the floor.

A white van was parked in the street outside. The robot opened the van's back door.

"Inside you two!" it commanded in its cold, metallic voice.

Back inside the bank, the robots had de-activated the extra security lock. They were now inside the bank's safe.

They were smashing open boxes filled with money.
They began to stuff the money into large steel crates.

"HURRY UP!" shouted the man in the grey suit.
"I want to be out of here in two minutes!"

The robots finished loading the crates.

They strode back into the main room of the bank, holding the steel crates in front of them.

"Back to the van!" shouted the man.

But at that second, a robot stamped into the bank, pushing Tyler in front of him.

"LEAVE ME ALONE!" yelled Tyler.

But the robot just held him tighter.

"IT IS TIME FOR THIS BOY TO DIE!" shouted the robot.

CHAPTER 5
OUT OF CONTROL

"GET HIM BACK IN THE VAN WITH THE GIRL!" screamed the man.

But the robot did not move.

The other four robots stood there holding their steel crates filled with money.

"I SAID GET HIM BACK TO THE VAN!"

Suddenly Tyler broke away from the robot and threw himself at the man.

The man toppled backwards and the flicker spun out of his hands.

It flew through the air and crashed onto the ground. The man and Tyler dived onto the floor, both reaching out for the flicker.

Tyler got there first but the man elbowed him out of the way.

The man's hand curled round the flicker and he jumped to his feet.

"Now I'm back in control!" he screamed with an evil laugh, aiming the flicker at the robot.

"NOW YOU WILL DO WHAT I SAY!"

The man pressed some buttons, but instead of doing what he commanded, the robot lunged forward and aimed a high kick at the man's chest.

He yelled out in pain and pressed the flicker again.

But the robot spun round and high kicked the flicker out of his hands.

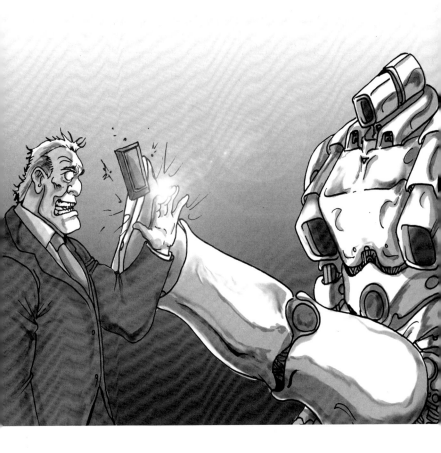

Then it lunged towards him, pushed

him over and sat on him.

At that second, armed police stormed the building.

They looked on in amazement at the scene in front of them.

The robot got to its feet.

All of the police officers raised their guns and aimed them at the robot.

"DON'T SHOOT!" yelled Tyler, running over and pulling off the robot's helmet.

"Thanks!" grinned Gail. "It was getting very hot in there!"

CHAPTER 6
THE PAY OFF

Two minutes later, Tyler and Gail were standing outside the bank.

They explained to the police officer in charge how they had overpowered the robot.

"It was empty inside the robot's body," said Gail, "so I climbed inside."

"She used her kick-boxing skills," added Tyler, "While I cut off the other robot's power."

"Incredible," replied the officer, "you did a great job in there."

He shook their hands and walked over
to join the other officers.

At that second Mum showed up. She
looked at the bank's smashed windows.

She stared at the armed officers who
were loading the gang of robots into a
large police van.

"What on earth has been going on here?" she demanded.

"I think you will need to go to another bank," said Tyler.

"Hey!" called one of the police officers. "We'll need that back!"
He pointed to the robot helmet under Gail's arm. She sighed and handed it over.

Tyler, Gail and Mum started walking down the street.

"What are you grinning about?" asked Tyler.

Gail held up a grey and blue sticky thing that looked like a small rugby ball.

"What is that?" asked Tyler.

"It's the robot's brain," grinned Gail, "it will be good for kick-boxing practice!"

Tyler laughed.

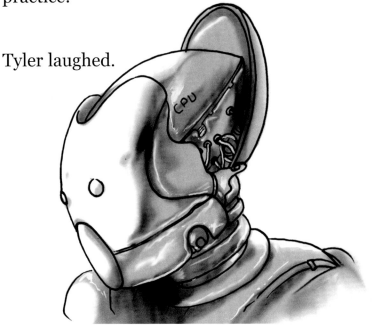

"Is one of you going to tell me what's going on?" demanded Mum.

"It's a long story," replied Tyler. "But if you get us a super size drink and a serious snack, we will tell you everything!"